SOW ? WHAT

SOW (*verb*)

1: to plant seed for growth, especially by scattering

2: to set something in motion: begin an enterprise

Girl Scouts of the USA

Chair,
National Board
of Directors

Connie L. Lindsey

Chief
Executive
Officer

Kathy Cloninger

Vice
President,
Program

Eileen Doyle

Girl Scouts.

WRITTEN BY Naomi Person

CONTRIBUTORS: Valerie Takahama,
Kathleen Sweeney, Rochana Rapkins

FRONT COVER by Aaron Kotowski

ILLUSTRATED BY Hadley Hooper and
Suzanne Stryk

DESIGNED BY Alexander Isley Inc.

EXECUTIVE EDITOR, JOURNEYS: Laura Tuchman

MANAGER, OPERATIONS: Sharon Kaplan

MANAGER, PROGRAM DESIGN: Sarah Micklem

Photographs

Page 2, back cover: © Aaron Kotowski;
Page 26: by John Sartin; **Page 32:**
©2008, Todd J. Martin (bakery); Rebecca
Blackwell/AP Images (Dakar market);
Page 38: ©Danita Delimont/Alamy;
Page 51: Mari Tefre/Global Crop Diversity
Trust; **Page 54:** Photo courtesy of the
Daily Local News, West Chester, PA;
Page 55: courtesy of Natural Lands
Trust; **Page 72:** courtesy of The Growing
Connection project (TGC); **Page 73:** by
Eric Ellingsen and Dickson Despommier;
Page 74: ©2006 Scott Hess; **Page 80:**
courtesy of Denise O'Brien; **Page 82:**
Danielle Stolman/Spartan Daily Staff;
Page 83: ©Plus One Pix/Alamy

Page 48: Excerpt from SILENT SPRING
by Rachel Carson. Copyright © 1962
by Rachel L. Carson, renewed 1990 by
Roger Christie. Used by permission of
Houghton Mifflin Harcourt Publishing
Company. All rights reserved.

© 2009 by Girl Scouts of the USA

First published in 2009 by Girl Scouts of the USA
420 Fifth Avenue, New York, NY 10018-2798
www.girlscouts.org

ISBN: 978-0-88441-735-4

Printed in Italy

2 3 4 5 6 7 8 9/17 16 15 14 13 12 11 10 09

Text printed on Fedrigoni Cento
40 percent de-inked, post-consumer
fibers and 60 percent secondary
recycled fibers.

Covers printed on Prisma artboard
FSC Certified mixed sources.

So, What's Inside?

Serving Size 96 pages

YOUR FOOD NETWORK

You probably know the Food Network, the cable channel where "Iron Chefs" do battle

and nearly everything edible has a time slot. But what about all the *other* food networks—the ones that connect you to everything you eat and everything your food eats and takes in for energy?

Each time you take a bite of something, whether an apple or a hamburger, you join a unique chain of food links. This chain can start with the sun or a food lab but then connects to the soil, a cow, a farmer, or a factory. But no matter how the chain links together, or how far it stretches, it always ends with you!

FOOD

FOOD connects you to the land where seeds sprout, to the water that irrigates crops, and to the oil that powers the planes and trucks that carry what you eat to you. Food production is affected by local laws and global markets, by workers' rights, and by climate change and weather. Food can be a pleasure—and a problem. Some people have enough food, some people have more than enough, and some have too little. It's been said that the world produces enough for everyone to be well fed, yet one person out of every eight doesn't get enough to eat. In fact, the poorest countries get 10 percent less food than what they need.

What can be done to even things out? This journey is an invitation to figure that out!

Some of you, and your families, may have gathered groceries for a food drive or donated money to an organization that fights hunger. Those are vital services—even more so in the face of an immediate crisis such as a hurricane or a fire. Long-lasting, sustainable change is something else altogether.

SOW WHAT

SOW WHAT will help you develop the leadership skills and confidence to create lasting change. As you explore innovative solutions, you'll be in good company. Across the country and around the world, girls and women are taking action to ensure that they, their families, and their neighbors have access to food that is healthful, affordable, and sustainably grown, which means it is produced with respect for the health of the planet and all who live on it.

Teens in Lubbock, Texas, are growing spinach, radishes, snow peas, and other nutrient-rich vegetables for a food bank that benefits many of their own families. The teens rotate crops to replenish the fertility of the fields.

Volunteers in California, Arizona, Idaho, and Massachusetts pick fallen fruit from parks and yards to feed women and children in domestic violence shelters, senior citizens, and others who have limited access to good food. Nearly 1.5 million pounds of grapefruits and oranges were harvested in one year in Phoenix alone!

In southern India, girls and women from the poorest economic class have come together to reclaim severely eroded cropland and to set up community grain funds so that when there is drought, they will still be able to feed the poorest of the poor. These girls and women also started their own radio station so that they could share their expertise and expand their reach.

The particulars of these projects differ, but the people behind them have one thing in common: They've joined together to address land use and food issues in their communities. They've researched and identified problems, discussed possible solutions, set goals, developed strategies, and followed through to create lasting change. Girls and women play a major role in the process. From New York City to New Delhi, from South America to Africa, girls and women usually bear the responsibility for feeding their families.

Sow What gives you the opportunity to have the same kind of influence. On this journey, you will CULTIVATE ideas by observing and analyzing various food needs and land-use issues in your community and in the world. You can use what you learn to PLANT the seeds that will lead to a more logical, sustainable, and environmentally sound HARVEST. The process of creating change is similar to a planting cycle: Each step makes the next one more fruitful.

As you travel along with your sister Girl Scouts, you'll have the option of earning this journey's distinguished Harvest Award. To earn it, here are the "seeds" of what you'll do:

Identify, and dig into, a food- or land-use issue, tapping some community experts as you go.

Capture your vision for change in a Harvest Plan that includes your very own "Sow What?"—your goal, why it matters, and how it will benefit both the planet and people.

Create change—execute your plan! How? By influencing a food policy or land-use effort (yes, you can!) or educating and inspiring others to act on a solution you identify.

The full details of these steps are found in the Harvest pages at the end of this book. As you review them, you will discover the possibility for lasting, significant change.

And as you wind your way through this journey, take time to enjoy your own food traditions with family, friends, and all the people you meet along the way. Those who grow food, study food, transport food, sell food, or cook food are bound to open your eyes to some delicious new career possibilities. Let them inspire you.

As you get a taste of all the topics in this journey, and what others around the world are doing about food and land issues, you'll be prepared (that's the Girl Scout motto!) to start thinking about how to improve your own food network and also the world's food network. You'll soon see that one is intimately tied to the other! When it comes to food and land use, there are plenty of ways to increase the bounty *and* educate and inspire everyone you know. Your Harvest project not only gives you a chance to contribute to the global food network, it might just add a whole new network to your life, too!

You've heard of the term "carbon footprint," right? It's the impact on the planet of all you do. Well, this journey will get you thinking about your "food print" and your "leader print." Sow your own definitions as you go!

MY FOOD PRINT =

MY LEADER PRINT =

FIVE FUN THINGS TO DO ALONG THE JOURNEY WITH FRIENDS, *especially Girl Scouts*

Plan a feast of local foods.

Better yet, shop for all your ingredients and then bring them to camp for a Sow What weekend of yummy meals and good conversation.

Talk about your values.

Sound corny? When do you really get to express who you are and what you stand for? Share what you value, hear what your friends value. Then, in a sisterly way, help one another live up to these values. (Check out all the women profiled along this journey. What are their values? How do they live them? Which of their values match your values?)

Imagine a future

you can sow for yourself. It may be quite different than you ever thought possible. What would it be like to be a scientist who invents a new way for people to grow food? A farmer who finds new ways to bring fresh foods to city markets? A chef who _____? An engineer who _____? Gather with your friends and go crazy! You never know where bright ideas will lead.

Find all the songs you can about food.

Get together and listen to or read the lyrics. So, what do you find?

Get dirty!

Just for fun, find something to plant—small or large. Enjoy the feel of soil in your hands, the smell of it in the air. Or simply go to a park and sit in the grass. Awaken all your senses in the great outdoors.

ARE YOU WHAT YOU EAT?

Just as you are part of a food network, the U.S. food system is part of a network, too.

Say you've got a burger on your plate. Where did it come from? Your fridge? A supermarket? A vending machine? A fast-food joint?

Most U.S. ingredients travel, on average, more than 1,500 miles before landing on your plate. Can you believe that? Your burger probably came from a cow raised in Texas, Kansas, or Nebraska. The tomato topping it likely came from Florida or Mexico. The more you know about where food comes from and how it reaches you, the more you'll understand the food network. Who knows? Maybe you'll be able to cultivate some positive changes that lessen your food print!

Researchers at the Leopold Center for Sustainable Agriculture in Iowa have traced the paths of 16 kinds of produce—from beans to potatoes to strawberries—that would typically end up on a supermarket shelf in the city of Des Moines. If they were grown in-state, their average "food miles" would be 56; if they were from other states, they might have to travel 1,494 miles—almost 27 times further! Then if you start to think globally about it, a bunch of grapes from Chile would have to be shipped by boat and then trucked an astounding 7,270 miles to reach the Midwest!

This is another way that food production connects to energy use, another gap in the food system into which gallons and gallons of gasoline are poured each year. Did you know, for example, that it takes more than 2,000 calories of fossil-fuel energy to make a one-calorie diet soda? Who do you think pays for all that gas? And at what cost to the environment?

Experts estimate that each person participating in the U.S. food system uses the equivalent of 500 gallons of gasoline a year, which is second only to the amount of gas Americans use in cars!

ZUCCHINI SQUASH
PRODUCT OF USA
1.59 $0.99
TOTAL PRICE
$1.57

Shopping the COOL Way

To reduce your food mileage, it's important to learn where
your food comes from. For reasons of health and food safety as
well, more and more consumers want that information. Cool!
Or rather, COOL! Country of Origin Labeling is a relatively new
federal regulation—a way for consumers to know where in the
world their fruits, vegetables, meats, and fish come from. A single
package of chopped meat can include beef from the United States,
Canada, and Mexico. In a supermarket, you may find farm-raised
shrimp from Thailand and wild shrimp from the Gulf of Mexico.
Your mangoes may come from Mexico and your garlic from China.

COOL labeling gives information about single ingredients, but
most processed foods include ingredients from multiple sources.
Even a single-serving can of apple juice, for example, might
include apples from Washington State, Belgium, and Ukraine.

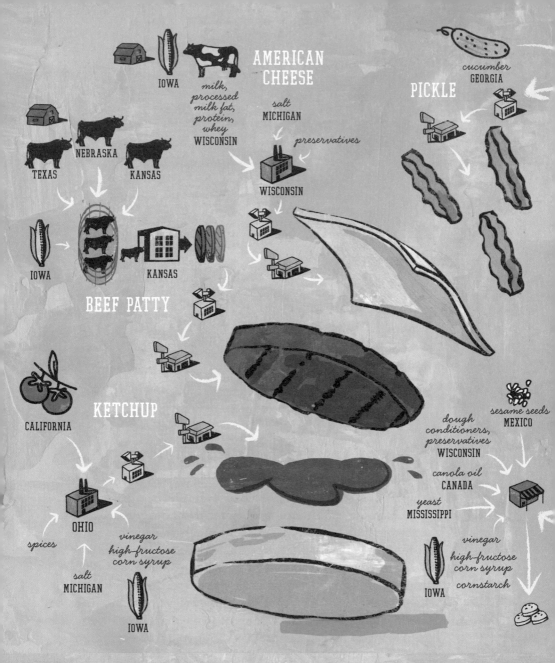

AMERICAN CHEESE

IOWA

milk, processed milk fat, protein, whey
WISCONSIN

salt
MICHIGAN

preservatives

WISCONSIN

PICKLE

cucumber
GEORGIA

TEXAS

NEBRASKA

KANSAS

IOWA

BEEF PATTY

KANSAS

KETCHUP

CALIFORNIA

OHIO

spices

salt
MICHIGAN

vinegar
high-fructose
corn syrup

IOWA

dough
conditioners,
preservatives
WISCONSIN

sesame seeds
MEXICO

canola oil
CANADA

yeast
MISSISSIPPI

vinegar
high-fructose
corn syrup
cornstarch

IOWA

The Food Print of a Burger

The average American eats 50 fast-food burgers each year. As a nation, that burger-eating habit is responsible for annual carbon emissions equal to that of 6.5 million SUVs. How is that possible? Take a look at how burger food miles add up!

Integrated Feedlot, Slaughterhouse, and Meat Processing Plant

natural flavoring

preservatives

salt
MICHIGAN

vinegar

NORTH CAROLINA

garlic powder

IOWA

colorings

TOMATO

FLORIDA

CALIFORNIA

LETTUCE

MUSTARD

wheat
KANSAS

mustard seeds
NORTH DAKOTA

turmeric
INDIA

MISSOURI

distilled white vinegar

BUN

IOWA

Corn and Products Made from Corn

Farm/Ranch

Factory

Mill

Bakery

Distribution Center

Fast Food Franchise

MAPPING YOUR PANTRY

Open your kitchen cabinets or visit a grocery store and check out the labels on a variety of single-ingredient goods. On your map, mark where you live and then put a dot on each country named on the labels. Connect the dots and you'll begin to see how your food choices connect you to the global food system.

What can you learn about the food networks of the countries that export food to us? What do people there eat? Do they have enough to eat? Who benefits most from each import-export relationship? Is Planet Earth the biggest loser?

With the planet in mind, go a step further: Since food miles gobble up energy, find out exactly how much energy your pantry consumes. On eatlowcarbon.org, the food service company Bon Appétit has devised a calculator that measures the amount of potential greenhouse gases emitted by various foods. Check it out and calculate your food impact.

Food	Energy Consumption

At the Market, Watch Your Step!

For many Americans, grocery stores and supermarkets are the primary link to fresh food. At most supermarkets, the healthiest way to shop is along the perimeter of the store. That's where fresh fruits and vegetables, fresh meat and seafood, and fresh dairy products are usually kept. The middle aisles are usually full of high-calorie, nutrient-poor snacks: chips, cookies, and sodas. Visit your supermarket and check out the perimeter. Now take stock of what parts of the store your family visits most. Map them out. If you find that lots of time is spent among sugar-coated cereals, corn-syrupy creations, and overprocessed products, create some new shopping rituals. Turn your walk around the store into a ritual! What marketing and advertising displays attract your attention? What advertising slogans might steer shoppers to healthier food?

19

STACY LEVY
The Food Web as Visual Art

As a sculptor, Stacy Levy admires the natural world not only for its outward beauty but also for the hidden patterns and processes that enable living things to grow and thrive.

Passing by a cornfield, for example, she thinks about the full story of corn—all the phases of its life cycle.

Levy is constantly exploring how we often think we know how something works or grows, but when we take a closer look we realize how much more there is to learn. In fact, even when driving by planted fields near her home in rural central Pennsylvania, she sometimes wonders, "What's that?" And then she realizes, "Oh, that's what food looks like when it's not in the supermarket!"

Levy makes giant, site-specific installations to illustrate some of the most amazing, but unnoticed, aspects of the world, including the food network. Most of her projects are large enough to walk around or on. Their creation and placement (at train stations, schools, public parks, and on city sidewalks) involve the collaboration of scientists, engineers, architects, and landscape architects.

Her aim is to reconnect things that have been separated in our modern world, sometimes by many miles, like the farm and the store. When people are at a supermarket, for example, Levy wants them to imagine the field where their vegetables grew. "How can you see where a carrot comes from?" she asks. "Do you carry it around with you? Do you walk your carrot to school 17 times, and every footstep signifies a mile on its journey from Salinas, Kansas, to Philadelphia, Pennsylvania?"

In summer, Levy narrows her food gap by growing a vegetable garden. But she finds herself spending most of her time weeding. "When you cultivate a garden, you're defending it more than anything else," she says. Defending, as Levy sees it, is nurturing: "You're giving your plants space and protecting them so that bigger things don't move in on their crib!"

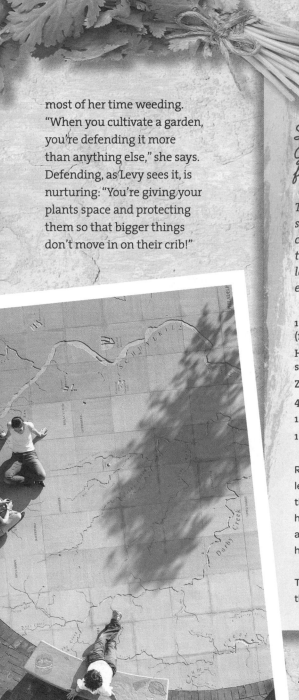

Stacy Levy's Garden Charmoula from Morocco

This recipe, Levy says, is "good for early spring or late fall, when parsley and cilantro are the only things growing in the garden. It is really made to go on lamb or fish, but it is great on anything except dessert."

1 cup parsley, washed and stems removed (flat Italian parsley works best)

Handful of cilantro, washed and stems removed

Zest of 1 lemon, chopped finely

4–6 tablespoons virgin olive oil

1/2 to 1 teaspoon sea salt

1 clove garlic, finely chopped

Roughly chop the parsley and cilantro leaves and place in a bowl. Mix in the rest of the ingredients. Let mixture sit, up to one hour, to allow the flavors to blend. If desired, add a pinch of chipotle pepper powder or hot paprika.

Toss with pasta, potatoes, lentils, or anything that needs some spicing up.

Stacy Levy's stone "Watermap" replicates part of the Delaware River watershed.

SHARI ROSE
Getting Kids to Eat Their Veggies

When Shari Rose became Youth Program Coordinator at the Brooklyn Rescue Mission in the Bedford-Stuyvesant neighborhood of Brooklyn, New York, she faced a lot of skepticism from the students she trained to work in the Mission's urban garden and at its farm stand.

"One boy didn't want to eat any vegetables," she recalls. "He said, 'If it was in the dirt, then it's dirty!' He hadn't seen any vegetable that wasn't on the supermarket shelves and that wasn't cleaned!"

When she'd ask the kids, "What is your favorite vegetable?" she'd hear things like: "I don't have one," "I hate tomatoes," and "I like broccoli but it has to be covered with cheese."

Rose understands how kids growing up in a neighborhood like Bed-Stuy, with few supermarkets and even fewer sources of fresh produce, might feel that way.

"Parents have to become role models," she says. "If they want their kids to eat healthy, then they themselves have to pass up that large order of french fries!"

Rose and her students spent early mornings and late afternoons in the garden, planting, weeding, composting, and sampling new tastes, including bitter melon. This long, bumpy vegetable is popular in Asian cuisine; it gets less bitter as it gets riper. The

Mission partnered with other food organizations to offer cooking demos, and the kids developed customer service and business skills by selling their produce at a strategically located farm stand, across from two bus stops and a subway station.

For Rose, the work was transformative. In October 2008, she spoke at a World Hunger Year event in New York, where she shared the stage with global economists, labor and farm organizers, and Alice Waters, the California chef whose name is synonymous with eating local, healthful foods.

Rose also attended nationwide conferences with other youth activists, and realized she is part of a movement of young people advocating for food justice.

"It's imperative that youth are given a voice, because youth are agents of change," she says. "It's important to be in charge of your nutrition."

So, what are Rose's favorite vegetables? Broccoli, cauliflower, and string beans.

During the summer, Shari Rose eats mainly from the garden. When she has enough prep time, she makes this sandwich and salad.

Tomato, Basil, Mozzarella Sandwich

1 tablespoon olive oil
1/2 teaspoon crushed garlic
Salt
Black pepper
1 large tomato, sliced
1 roll (preferably a French bread roll), cut open
4 ounces fresh mozzarella cheese, sliced
1 cup fresh basil

In a small container, mix olive oil, garlic, salt, and pepper to taste. Layer the tomato slices on half of the roll, then add the cheese. Place the basil on top. Pour the oil mixture over the open sandwich and then place the other piece of roll on top. Cut in half and enjoy.

Easy Peach and Mint Salad

4 fresh peaches, cubed
1/2 cup fresh mint
1/2 teaspoon cinnamon
1/2 tablespoon brown sugar

Combine all ingredients in a bowl. Chill the salad in the refrigerator for at least 30 minutes and then serve.

The Local Dining Scene

Many organizations promote eating local—that is, eating foods grown close to where you live. If you buy from farmers, bakeries, and other homegrown markets, you decrease your food miles and your energy footprint. And you increase your flavor potential. The minute something is picked, its cells start to break down. So the quicker you pop a fresh-picked peach into your mouth, the more intense the flavor is. It will also be higher in nutrients—the vitamins, minerals, and proteins that nourish your body. Take note: Nutrients also fuel your brain! That's right, the more well-nourished you are, the better you will think and learn!

There's also an economic argument for eating locally: The money you spend "buying local" keeps small farms in your region healthy. If you buy in a supermarket, the farmer gets only about 20 cents for every dollar you spend. At a farmers' market, you can quadruple the amount going to the farmer.

Try being a locavore! For a week, or longer, ask your family to limit its food purchases to items produced within a 100-mile radius of your home. What amazing meals can you create with only local food? Keep a log of them. Are you enjoying them? Are you missing anything by eating local?

SOMETHING TO CHEW ON

To eat or not to eat . . . local, organic, or conventionally grown? That is the question. A local apple may have been grown with some sort of pesticide, but it hasn't been shipped cross-country to reach you. Organic strawberries at a New York supermarket in January may not have had any fossil fuel–based fertilizer dumped on them, but they've traveled all the way from California in the dead of winter. What's the better choice? Is there one? Or is it a matter of weighing priorities and practical considerations such as convenience and affordability? How might you find a balance?

Figuring out where you stand on these issues gets at the heart of your food print—and the choices you can make to change it.

What's Ripe for the Picking?

The Natural Resources Defense Council has a great way to find out what fruits and vegetables are in season in your area. Just visit nrdc.org/health/foodmiles. Enter the name of your state and the month and you'll receive the information, along with recipes.

BARBARA EISWERTH
No Fruit Tree Left Behind

Barbara Eiswerth uses mapping software to locate year-round treasure in backyard gardens. The bounty? Peaches, pomegranates, citrus, and more.

In the mountain-ringed desert city of Tucson, Arizona, fruit trees produce prodigiously. But they are often planted for ornamental purposes only. Their fruit drops to the ground uneaten. "We transport food to markets thousands of miles away and let it rot in our own backyards," says Eiswerth. Her favorite tree, the lemon, produces up to 3,000 fruits per year.

A former Girl Scout (in Pennsylvania), Eiswerth put her Ph.D. in Arid Lands Resource Management to work by coaxing property owners and commercial farmers to join in creating a database of gleanable trees whose fruit could benefit Tucson's neediest residents. Eiswerth calls her project the Iskash*taa Refugee Harvest Network.

*Iskash*taa* is Somali for "working cooperatively together." Tucson's many refugees from war-torn Somalia provided a willing group of former farmers to collect and distribute the fruit. The project now brings together refugees from several countries, students, retirees, church members, hydroponic growers, and social workers to rescue 30,000 pounds of produce. Its motto? No fruit tree left behind!

The project also offers "Fun with Fruit" events—how-tos for making lemonade with pomegranate, prickly pear, and calamansi, and tips for cooking with loquats, kumquats, and olives. "Food is such a common denominator, it bridges communities," Eiswerth says.

Eiswerth presented her harvesting plan at a Faith-Based and Community Initiatives Roundtable in 2008. Her documentary, "Iskash*taa: An Invitation to Community," won a Department of Health and Human Services "Portraits of Compassion" award.

Roasted Pumpkin Seeds

Separate the fiber from the pumpkin seeds. Place the seeds in a colander and rinse thoroughly with water.

Place the seeds in a saucepan and cover with 2 quarts water. Add 1/4 cup salt if desired. Bring the seeds to a boil and simmer about 2 hours. Drain the seeds and dry them on absorbent paper.

Preheat oven to 300 degrees. Place seeds in a shallow pan. Sprinkle with hot chili pepper, lime juice, onion, or garlic salt if desired. Roast in the oven for 30 to 40 minutes or until golden brown. Stir occasionally.

Remove the seeds from the oven and add one teaspoon of melted butter to each cup of seeds. If not seasoned, salt to taste. When cool, store in an airtight container. If longer than 10 to 14 days, store in the freezer.

The Great Pumpkin Plan

Barbara Eiswerth also helps rescue nutritious pumpkins from post-Halloween decay. She collaborates with Girl Scouts and other youth groups to collect and distribute the fruit along with recipes. Here's her plan:

1. **Contact farmer of local pumpkin patch for permission to glean unused pumpkins.**

2. **Once you have permission, set up gleaning dates.**

3. **Record owner's name, address, telephone, and e-mail.**

4. **Devise plan to store and/or redistribute the pumpkins.**

5. **Harvest the pumpkins (be sure you have a team!).**

6. **Donate/distribute whole pumpkins with recipe cards.**

Location, Location, Location

Terroir (pronounced tehr-WAHR) is a French word that means "taste of the place." In Europe, various geographic regions associated with producing a particular kind of food are reserved for just that. For example, balsamic vinegar comes from the Modena region in Italy. Kalamata olives are from Greece. There are more than 750 "place-based" foods in Europe, where *terroir* is used to market a product.

In the United States, Vidalia onions are grown only in Georgia; Walla Walla sweet onions grow in Walla Walla County, Washington, and in northeastern Oregon. Vermont maple syrup producers are also exploring a special designation because, they say, a syrup's flavor is tied to the soil in which a maple tree is grown. And in Iowa, agricultural researchers are hoping to revive the popularity of watermelons and cantaloupes grown in Muscatine County on the banks of the Mississippi River. Researchers say that these melons get their sweet, intense flavor from the glacial soil and a long, warm growing season.

THE SOW WHAT OF SOIL

Soils, like accents, are distinctive and a product of their geography. The National Cooperative Soil Survey, part of the U.S. Department of Agriculture, has identified and mapped more than 20,000 kinds of soil in the United States.

Soil names include root syllables that provide clues to the soils' traits: *Glac*, Latin for icy, like a glacier, means there are ice wedges in the soil; *Hal*, Greek for salt, means the soil is salty; and *Hydr*, from the Greek *hydr*o or water, means H_2O is present.

What kind of soil do you have near where you live? What grows in it? Find an unused patch of soil and dig out a cupful. What does it feel like?

Here are some words that are used to classify soil: sandy, which is gritty; silt, which is somewhat fluffy like flour; and clay, which is thick and wet. Can you see anything alive in your soil? Bring it to your next Girl Scout gathering. Compare it to soil that your sister Seniors have dug up.

WHAT'S YOUR *Terroir?*

In what ways are the tastes of local foods tied to the region where you live, and to its soil? Don't know? Talk to someone who does. It might be fun to ask out-of-state relatives, too. What foods are unique to their region? What soils?

SIV LIE
Cooking with and for People

When Siv Lie founded the Boston University chapter of Slow Food, a movement based on the principle that everyone has the right to good food and the pleasures of eating, she devised a direct approach to engage her peers: "Hey, do you like food?" she'd ask everyone passing by the table she'd set up in the student union.

Next to her placards, she'd have muffins, breads, and local cheeses, which she offered for free. "The only catch was once they got their food they had to sit down," says Lie. And then, of course, they'd talk. Lie would pepper the conversation with questions about what they ate, where they bought it, and how and with whom they cooked it.

At BU, Lie developed a relationship with a manager of a small dining hall and together they introduced "trayless Tuesdays." This forced students to carry their food, which meant they would take less and waste less.

Lie grew up with a strong appreciation for food, especially foods traditional to her family, like the goat cheese she shared with her Norway-born father. In college, she designed her own major combining anthropology and food culture. During her junior year abroad in France, she connected with Slow Food and had a chance to meet one of its co-founders, Carlo Petrini.

"I thought, 'He is so important, he'll never talk to me,'" she recalls. But she mustered the courage to approach him and he agreed to sit with her and answer her questions. "I recorded his voice for 15 minutes," she says, "and when I saw him a year and a half later at the Slow Food Nation gathering [in San Francisco], he recognized me!"

Inspired by Petrini, Lie now says the most important way to be part of change is through personal action. An ideal way to educate people about food, she adds, is to have a cooking party where everyone brings an ingredient. "Make the time to come home and cook with people," she says. "It's a great way to be involved in the food system!"

Party Time!

Follow Siv Lie's advice for a cooking party: Get each of your Senior friends to bring one ingredient and see what you can cook up. What ingredients arrived? What did you decide to make? How did it taste?

Savory-Sweet Acorn Squash

In this recipe, Siv Lie doesn't measure the honey or oil. Cooks, she says, should learn to trust their judgment and estimate. Not bad advice for life, too!

2 acorn squash
Olive oil
1 tablespoon coarsely chopped fresh rosemary or 1 teaspoon dried rosemary
Salt and pepper for seasoning
Honey (optional)

Preheat oven to 400 degrees.

Slice each squash in half lengthwise and scoop out the seeds. Place each half on a cutting surface, skin side up. Cut each half into chunks about one-inch square. Arrange squash chunks on a cookie sheet, skin side down.

For sweeter squash, mix one part honey to two parts olive oil. Otherwise use olive oil only. Brush or spoon onto squash to coat. Then sprinkle with rosemary, salt, and pepper.

Roast in oven for 40–50 minutes, until tender.

LOCAL FOODS AROUND THE WORLD

The *Inuit of Northern Quebec* eat seal and whale meat, caribou, and salmon, known as *niqituinnaq*, "really food" in Inuktitut. Whale meat is high in beneficial fatty acids—and dangerous levels of chemicals. *Akutaq*, an Inuit "ice cream," is made of game fat, seal oil, fish and fish oil, snow, and fresh berries.

Thailand's many curry dishes feature freshwater and saltwater fish simmered with vegetables in coconut milk, chilies, ginger, and cilantro. In some impoverished areas, rice is the bulk of the diet.

In *Japan*, high food costs are offset by the fact that 84 percent of meals are eaten at home. A typical meal is miso soup, *yakizakana* (grilled fish), steamed rice, braised bok choy, and pickled vegetables.

German families spend as much as $500 a week on food. A traditional meal is *Bratwurst mit Kartoffeln und Sauerkraut* (sausages with potatoes and sauerkraut). Bakeries abound in major cities.

In *Senegal*, droughts and large families mean that malnutrition is high. *Thiéboudienne* (marinated fish with eggplant, carrots, and sweet potatoes over rice) is a traditional dish. *Jus de bissap* is a drink of boiled hibiscus flowers with lemon, sugar, and mint.

In *Venezuela*, nearly a fifth of the population lives on less than a dollar a day. *Pabellón criollo* is a common dish of rice, black beans, and shredded beef served with fried plantains. *Arepas* (corn cakes) and *batidos* (fruit smoothies made from mangoes, papayas, and guava) are popular.

In *Honduras*, corn tortillas are a staple. *Fresco natural* (natural juice) is a key part of the main meal—usually lunch. People make their own juice; tamarind and raspberries are popular. Special-occasion dishes include *carne asada* (grilled beef) and *baleadas,* flour tortillas with beans, *crema* (cream), and/or cheese.

Of all the world's citizens, Americans spend the smallest percentage of their total income on food.

United States, 9.8%
Canada, 11.3%
Germany, 15%
Japan, 23%
Thailand, 26%
Honduras, 30%
Venezuela, 41%
Inuit of Quebec, 50%
Senegal, 53%

Orlando Sierra / AFP / Getty Images

How Close Is Your Food?

As the world's population expands, more and more people are moving to cities. The United Nations estimates that half the world's population now lives in urban areas, far from the rural areas where most food is produced.

People from very different cultures are also eating the same foods. Many societies have switched from cereals and grains as their main source of protein to animal products. In short, they've shifted from low-calorie, nutrient-rich food to calorie-dense, nutrient-poor food. They're also eating more processed food, which not only lacks key nutrients but also lacks any connection to a society's culture and traditions. As food becomes disconnected from history and heritage, people's lives lose something, too.

The popularity of processed foods has also led to a more tangible problem: rising obesity rates. It may be hard to believe, but more people in the world are overweight than hungry. The rate of obesity is growing fastest among young people. If nothing is done, future generations will likely face increasing risks of diabetes, heart ailments, and high blood pressure. Some people are already on alert. In Philadelphia, city officials have moved to limit food advertising to children, especially in schools.

"Make the time to come home and cook with people. It's a great way to be involved in the food system!"
—SIV LIE

I'm Hungry, Now!

So many of us—young people and adults—
complain that we just don't have time for all we
want to do. That often makes fast food and other
prepackaged and processed snacks a staple in
our lives. What food habits do you slip into for
convenience? Do you also enjoy those foods?
What would entice you to make different food
choices, even ones that required more of your
time and attention?

WHAT'S FOR LUNCH?

Think of a bowl of brown rice versus a bowl
of potato chips. Which will give you the
most energy to, say, walk to a friend's
house or study for school? Keep a
tally of your lunches for a week or
two. What are you eating? Did you
make your food or buy it? Are you
seeing any patterns? How about corn in
its many forms? Is it in your lunch?

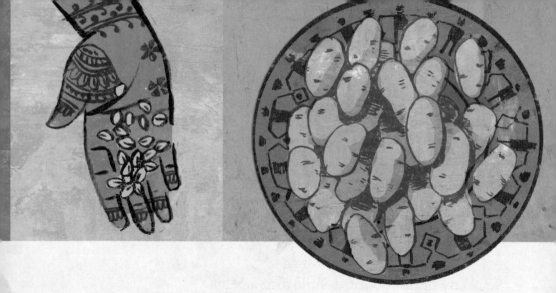

HONOR THY FOOD

Societies around the world honor food traditions and growing cycles with ceremonies for planting, harvesting, and sharing the crops. In many cultures, a strong spiritual connection to food is passed from generation to generation.

In India, for example, special days are chosen to start preparing the fields, sowing the seeds, and reaping the harvest. The women hold ceremonies to mark the arrival of the grain at the threshing yard. They pray for seeds going into winter storage and for a good crop in the next growing season, and before seeds are sown, they are worshipped.

In the Indian region of Ladakh, nestled beneath the Himalayas, community members have a special ritual before meals. They close their eyes to give thanks for their food and to honor each person involved in creating the meal before them.

Iranians celebrate the Persian New Year, or the Nowruz Spring Festival, by serving seven dishes. Each starts with the Persian letter "s," and each represents one of the "angelic heralds of life." *Sabzeh*, or sprouts, stands for rebirth and fertility. *Samanu,* a pudding, symbolizes the sweetness of life. *Sib* is an apple, which represents beauty and health. *Senjed,* the dried fruit of a wild olive or lotus

tree, symbolizes love. *Seer,* garlic, represents medicine and healing. *Somaq,* sumac berries, represents the sunrise and the belief that good conquers evil. And *serkeh,* vinegar, represents age and patience.

In the United States, some families say grace before eating. But busy schedules have made family meals less common. One out of every five meals is now eaten in a car. Ask adults in your family about their experience as kids. What lively conversations, interesting debates, or laughable moments came up at the dinner table?

"Food is such a common denominator, it bridges communities."

—BARBARA EISWERTH

BRINGING HOME THE HARVEST

In the Peruvian village of Aymara, which holds an annual potato celebration at harvesttime, women learn about potatoes from their parents and grandparents. Each year they sort through hundreds of potatoes to figure out which to eat, sell, trade, or use for seed.

Imagine living so close to food and being so involved in its growing that you, too, would be able to sense how it will taste and how its seeds will grow just by holding and studying it.

An offering of potatoes at the Inti Raymi Festival in Cusco, Peru

New Ritual for a New Day

Create a ritual that honors what you eat. Start with a food that you love. Research everything you can about it: where it originated, traditional preparation, where it's currently grown, who picks or produces it. Use what you've learned to create a collage, a short essay or photo essay, or a video. Share it with other Girl Scouts and with your community.

Fun with Food Festivals

Are your food festivals limited to the street fair variety or does your family have festivals it celebrates each year? Festivals, holidays, and other celebrations almost always involve food. What foods take the cake at your family's rituals and gatherings? What are your favorites? And what's your favorite food festival? If you don't have one, dream one up! Create a food festival of your own, featuring your ideal foods.

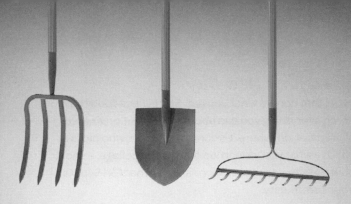

THEN AND NOW

Now that the food network is simmering in your brain, it's time to add in some history and current events.

This is the dirt to really dig into to see the role your food print plays in the larger food web. After all, humans have been growing food for some 12,000 years. We've been gathering it and eating it for far longer. The survival of our species depends upon it.

So how did this basic and vital part of life get to be at the center of so many challenging contemporary issues, including conservation of energy, climate change, economic development, equal rights, and the humane treatment of all living organisms?

The answers are complex. In a way, the history of food is like a frame that you can move backward and forward in time to get a snapshot of local, national, and global situations.

SO, WHAT GOT US HERE?

In the middle of the last century, the way our country produced food changed dramatically, and along with it so did the rest of our culture—and our environment and our international relationships.

In 1945, when World War II ended, the U.S. government had a surplus of ammonium nitrate, a chemical used in making bombs. Ammonium nitrate contains nitrogen, which is one of the key nutrients and biological building blocks for plants and animals. In nature, nitrogen is produced in the soil from sources such as bacteria, decaying crops, and manure, which is a tried-and-true fertilizer. In traditional agriculture, when crops use up the nitrogen in a field, that field will be sown with other plants that can replenish the nitrogen over the course of a few years.

Nitrogen has always been a "limiting factor" in agriculture; you need it to grow crops, but you have to wait for nature to replenish it in the soil. Scientists realized they could process the surplus ammonium nitrate and "fix," or remove, the nitrogen, which could then be used as fertilizer. Keeping nitrogen coming meant increased crop yields.

But to fix nitrogen, nitrogen and hydrogen must be put under great pressure. This process is powered by electricity, the majority of which is fueled by coal, a fossil fuel and therefore a nonrenewable resource. As fertilizer use expanded over the years, other sources took prominence over ammonium nitrate. The crop that benefited most from these new chemical fertilizers was corn, which had already been bred so that it could be planted very close together. Chemical fertilizers made sure that those crowded cornfields could keep producing. This was the start of the industrialization of agriculture.

Growing More of Less: Monoculture

Remember the model of American agriculture portrayed in the song "Old MacDonald Had a Farm"? A family farm where cows, chickens, and other livestock grazed not far from fruit orchards and fields of corn, potatoes, and tomatoes? In just a few decades, American agriculture has narrowed so that most farmers now specialize in vast acres of only one or two crops, most often corn and soy.

The practice of growing one crop in huge quantities is called monoculture. In the United States, more than 80 percent of cropland is now devoted to monocultures of corn, wheat, soy, and hay. These crops, especially corn and soy, are used to feed cows, pigs, and sheep at big factory farms because it is cheaper and faster than letting the animals graze naturally. Corn also shows up in everything from cereal to soda, as cheap-to-produce sweeteners such as corn syrup, fructose, and malt dextrose. Corn sweeteners are full of calories but have almost no nutrients, causing some critics to argue that they shouldn't be added to our food.

Also, scientists have figured out how to convert corn and other foods into fuel for cars and machinery. Farmers worldwide are getting paid to grow thousands of acres of crops to be used for fuel instead of food. In this way, food crops will become more and more a part of the global economy.

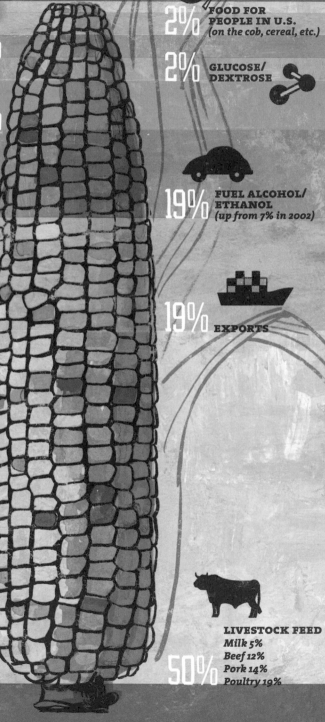

BEVERAGE ALCOHOL **1%**

CORN STARCH **2%**

HIGH-FRUCTOSE CORN SYRUP **5%**

2% **FOOD FOR PEOPLE IN U.S.**
(on the cob, cereal, etc.)

2% **GLUCOSE/ DEXTROSE**

19% **FUEL ALCOHOL/ ETHANOL**
(up from 7% in 2002)

19% **EXPORTS**

The Many Uses of U.S. Corn

Corn comes in many forms—corn on the cob, creamed corn, popcorn, corn chips. With corn-fed poultry, corn-fed cows, and corn-fed farmed fish, the corn content of the U.S. diet can reach 58 percent. That includes high-fructose corn syrup, a key ingredient in chewing gum, sodas, fruit drinks, and snack foods of all sorts. It's also in hot dogs, margarine, and mayonnaise. And then there's corn starch, a thickener and anticaking agent.

Add in all the nonfood uses of corn—disposable diapers to shoe polish, firecrackers to biofuel . . . the list goes on! Basically, we live in a corn-centric universe.

LIVESTOCK FEED
Milk 5%
Beef 12%
Pork 14%
Poultry 19%

50%

ANCIENT WAYS, MODERN TIMES

White corn is central to the creation story of the Tsyunhehkwa, part of the Oneida Nation of Iroquois in Wisconsin. Each summer, the Tsyunhehkwa hold a Green Corn festival to celebrate the whiter, milkier, sweeter version of the corn. And every fall they burn tobacco to honor and recognize the corn and everyone involved in its cultivation. Seeds from the plants that demonstrate the best attributes—eight kernel rows, one ear per stalk—are saved. A community harvest follows in which white corn is snapped and husked, and the husks are braided. In their own cannery, the Tsyunhehkwa process and produce raw corn, dehydrated corn, corn soup, corn bread, and corn flour—everything but corn syrup, the highly processed sweetener that has become a cash cow of modern industrial agriculture.

COUNT YOUR KERNELS

List what you eat on an average couple of days. What plants and animals are involved? What processed foods are you eating? Keep a label log of them and count how many contain some form of corn. Which form of corn crops up the most? So, what does that tell you?

Trade lists with a sister Girl Scout who is also on this journey. What advice can you offer each other? Maybe you can set some goals together. And while you're at it, bite into this: Why is it that what's good for the planet is often what's good for you, too?

CORN

Able to adapt to extreme climates, this New World native now grows in more places around the world than any other grain. Its botanical name, *Zea mays*, comes from *zea*, Greek for grain, and *mais*, a Haitian Indian word meaning "the stuff of life." By the time Columbus sailed the ocean blue, more than 200 types of corn were being grown by Native Americans.

FROM VARIETY TO THE BIG 3

When you think of all the countries, languages, geographies, and traditions in the world, it makes sense that there would also be endless varieties of food. But given the rise in monocultures, one in every five calories eaten in the world today is rice. Rice, corn, and wheat make up 60 percent of the world's food.

Nobody set out to diminish biodiversity. But monocultures choke out native plants, which are suited to particular growing conditions. The loss of one native plant can trigger an ecological domino effect. For example, increasing corn acreage to produce ethanol for fuel can increase soil erosion, which in turn decreases the number of natural predators that control pests in neighboring soybean fields.

The concept of biodiversity was first put forth by E. O. Wilson, a preeminent scientist, global conservationist, and the world's foremost expert on ants. Biodiversity refers to all the varieties of life in a given area. That area can be as small as your backyard or as big as a forest, an ocean, or Earth. Biodiversity is like a thread that stretches from the beginning of life on Earth to the present. The big issue for scientists working in the field of biodiversity is how far into the future these threads, teeming with life, will extend.

Wilson wants to catalog as much information about species as possible. There may be between 30 million and 100 million species on the planet, but only 1.6 million have been identified. And believe it or not, just 15 plant species and eight animal species account for 90 percent of our food.

Wilson has partnered with several scientific and educational institutions to start an online Encyclopedia of Life. He also launched the BioBlitz, a large-scale, daylong community audit of biodiversity, in which volunteers record information and bring samples to scientists for identification and data entry. The goals of the BioBlitz are twofold: to add to existing species lists as much as possible and also to increase public awareness of biodiversity and the fact that it can exist in even the tiniest environment.

> *"The balance of nature is ... a complex, precise, and highly integrated system of relationships between living things which cannot be safely ignored any more than the laws of gravity can be defied."*
> —RACHEL CARSON

Your Own BioBlitz

A great way to see and appreciate the diversity around you is to conduct your own BioBlitz. Whom could you partner with to plan one in your community? What locations would you survey? No need to go all day— how about a half-day blitz?

POTATOES

There are 4,500 potato varieties in the world, 3,000 of them from Peru, where the Incas were their first cultivators. Round, twisted, and spiraled, the varieties have ancient Andean names that include "like a deer's white tongue" and "makes the daughter-in-law cry." Potatoes were the first food grown in space—aboard the shuttle *Columbia*.

BANK ON IT!

One way to preserve biodiversity is to save seeds. The government of Norway has opened a Global Seed Vault near the Arctic Circle that is designed to hold samples of 4.5 million seeds, as a way to safeguard them. It has been described as a Noah's Ark for securing biological diversity for future generations. Another way to preserve biodiversity is to restore habitats by reintroducing native plants.

Diversity and You

The natural world thrives on diversity. When in your own life has diversity improved things? Instead of food, think about music. Think of all the influences that come together in the music you love. What if there were only one kind of music? Not such a great idea, huh? What diversity do you see around you—at school, where you shop, where you worship? Where do you see efforts to create and maintain diversity? What obstacles do you see? What network could you start through Girl Scouting to get more people mixing it up? What other Girl Scout Seniors are in your region? What are they up to? Check in with your Girl Scout council and cultivate your network! Think about how rich your harvest could be!

LYDIA SOMERS AND IVY VANCE
Restoring Iowa Prairies

Experts estimate that, across the Great Plains, less than 1 percent of the original prairie remains. Lydia Somers and Ivy Vance, two Girl Scouts from North Liberty, Iowa, decided to restore one patch of prairie in a barren lot behind their town's elementary school.

"It wasn't even remotely prairielike," says Ivy. "It was just a big, open space, so we had to cut down a lot of trees and stuff because trees don't really grow in the prairie. There were a lot of invasive species, too, like ragweed."

The girls planted native species such as black-eyed Susans, milkweed, and tall prairie grass. "We would mix seed with large bags of sand," explains Lydia, "and then scatter that across the prairie and use rakes to kind of turn it into the soil."

The duo, both high school students, mobilized members of their Troop 1076 for the original weeding and planting. Then they maintained the prairie by volunteering a few hours of their time each week. "If you just know to split up the work," says Ivy, "two people can really get it done."

With their patch of prairie now thriving, they plan to mentor younger girls in prairie maintenance. "It's habitat to a lot of animals," says Lydia. "You see coyotes, rabbits.... It's important to preserve it. Seeing the results is really what keeps you going."

"If you start with something small," Ivy adds, "you can always make it bigger."

"I think this one will keep us busy for a while," says Lydia. "We were amazed the first year the flowers grew. And we were so happy with it that I think I may do more things like this."

MOLLY MORRISON
Listening to the Land

Molly Morrison loves to visit nature preserves just to listen. "When you are outdoors and walking in a preserve, you get to carefully listen and distinguish the sounds—of a bird or a cricket, or the sound of the water in a creek," she says. "I can't identify the songs of many birds. But that doesn't matter. What matters to me is being part of this natural experience."

As president of the Natural Lands Trust, Morrison also uses her listening skills to preserve the natural beauty of rolling farmlands, tidal marshes, wildflower meadows, and other open spaces in the greater Philadelphia region.

Land trusts are organizations that help protect land from development. They work with farmers, ranchers, nonprofits, and other property owners, and with towns and other public entities to negotiate agreements restricting development and other activities on parcels of land.

The agreements, known as "conservation easements," apply to all future owners of the property. That way, the land is permanently protected.

Once the land is protected, it must also be cared for and managed, and, in some cases, restored to its natural state. Some land trusts work toward controlling invasive plants, reintroducing native plants, and managing for native wildlife species such as birds, butterflies, and a variety of animals.

The Natural Lands Trust, founded in 1953, owns and manages more than 40 nature preserves covering more than 20,000 acres in Pennsylvania and New Jersey. It's one of about 1,600 U.S. land trusts.

"No matter where you are, there's probably a land trust nearby," Morrison says. Land trusts vary in size. Some are focused on a particular town or a branch of a river.

So to enjoy nature, "you don't have to go to a national park," Morrison says. "Sometimes the best experiences with nature are those nearby— often within drivable, or even walkable, distances."

Being One with the Land (Trust)

Feel like getting outside? How about getting dirty? Take some time for an outdoor adventure with friends, maybe even in a land trust near you. To find one, visit lta.org, and click on Find a Land Trust Near You.

How do you feel when you connect with nature? How do you feel when you return home?

SUZANNE STRYK
Sharing an Awe for Nature

In grade school, Suzanne Stryk was a self-described clock-watcher, always waiting for the bell to ring so she could run outdoors. There she'd watch robins tilt their heads, look at the earth, and then pull up a worm. "I knew then, though I couldn't express it, that they were experts at living," she says.

Her exploration of the natural world grew into a love of biology and art, and inspired an excitement for her academic studies. She began to see how certain human actions were harming the planet. Then, when she was 15, she read a book

called *The Immense Journey,* by Loren Eiseley. It changed her life.

"He made me realize that people had the ability to reflect upon the natural world in a way no other species can," says Stryk. "So the visual arts were my way of cultivating my awareness of nature. Drawing, which had begun as a sort of hobby, became a way of fulfilling that deep awareness of the natural world."

Styrk is fascinated by how things grow, and the nitty-gritty toil of microorganisms in the soil. Her art, often made with plant stains—coffee, tea, walnuts, and pokeberries—is part of a larger dialogue.

"My work puts us in the great evolutionary story of life on earth as observers and meaning-makers," she says. "My images don't simply describe the way an animal looks, but rather they explore how we *perceive* the animal. I guess it all boils down to my wanting to share respect and awe for *all* creatures, which includes humans and their special role as witnesses to the living world."

"Down to Earth" by Suzanne Stryk, watercolor with plant stains, acrylic, pencil, gesso, and ink on paper.

Get Creative With Food

When you think of all the senses involved in eating—smell, touch, hearing, and taste, especially taste—you realize how many chances you have each day to make discoveries!

Once you've made a discovery, there are many ways to express what it means to you. Go outside and pay attention to the textures and sounds of the natural world and take inspiration from them. Explore something about food or the land, agricultural workers, or urban farmers that moves you. Create a work of art, in any medium. If it makes a strong statement about change, share it with others.

THE DIRT ON SOIL

Let's talk some more about dirt.

You don't want to grind it into the carpet or smear it on your jeans. But dirt, in its fullest and most organic form, is a substance that supports life.

Soil is full of nutrients that make seeds grow. Those nutrients include nitrogen, phosphorous, calcium, and sodium, substances that feed the plants that feed us. Soil is like a stored energy pack. But as with any battery, it doesn't have an endless power supply. It needs to recharge!

Farmers do that by using a few time-tested techniques: They rotate crops to avoid having the same one growing on the same acreage year after year. And they use "cover" crops.

Every autumn at Hawthorne Valley Farm, a community-supported agriculture (CSA) enterprise in upstate New York, rye and clover are planted on fields that won't be used for commercial crops such as broccoli, peas, and kale for another 18 months. During that downtime, the long roots of the rye grass burrow deep into the dirt to aerate the soil. The clover replenishes nutrients, especially nitrogen; it's a natural fertilizer.

There are also armies of animals and bacteria at work. Worms wiggle around in the soil to open up spaces for air and for optimal water uptake. In just a handful of topsoil, microscopic bugs number in the billions. Weigh out a pound of dirt and the unseen bugs within it will far outnumber Earth's human population of more than 6.7 billion.

Another issue with soil is keeping it in place. Land development, cutting down trees for lumber, and overgrazing by animals flattens soil that should be spongy and productive. Strong winds and heavy rains also blow and wash away stressed soils, a process known as erosion. The United States is losing soil 20 times faster than it can be naturally replaced. In other countries, such as China and India, the rates of soil loss are 30 and 40 times faster.

Erosion also washes any chemical fertilizers in the soil into water-sheds and the ocean, creating "dead zones," where fish and other organisms cannot survive. In the Gulf of Mexico, into which the Mississippi River flows, the dead zone was, in 2008, larger than the state of Massachusetts!

MUSHROOMS
Not Just Pizza Topping

If you want to turn an empty lot into a garden, how do you ensure that the soil is clean? One scientist who has studied mushrooms for more than 30 years says that fungi, the biological classification to which mushrooms belong, are the real pros of soil cleaning.

Fungi, of which mushrooms are the fruit, grow long underground cells known as mycelia that produce enzymes and acids that break down plant matter, including chains of hydrogen and carbon molecules. They can even break down the hydrocarbon chains of petroleum products, including pesticides and other chemicals.

Mycologist Paul Stamets did an experiment in which several mounds of dirt were contaminated with diesel fuel. In the dirt pile where oyster mushroom spores had been introduced, after eight weeks, 95 percent of the hydrocarbons had been broken down, meaning most of the oil residue was gone. Flies that are attracted to mushrooms, known as fungus gnats, ate the spores. The gnats attracted other insects and birds, which brought in seeds. The seeds, in turn, meant regrowth.

Stamets, a former logger, is a champion of preserving old-growth forests, where fungi thrive. He contends that saving these forests is a matter of national defense because fungi can break down the compounds found in chemical weapons. He also says that mycelium "mats" can be used to stem erosion, and they possess certain antibiotic and antiviral properties that are just beginning to be explored.

Fungi are an example of how an entire community can be more efficient in a task than any one organism. You may never think of a mushroom as just another salad or pizza ingredient again.

WHEAT covers more of Earth's surface—
about 500 million acres—than any other crop.
Ground into flour, wheat is most often the main
ingredient in bread, "the staff of life." About 15
percent of the world's wheat is grown in Pakistan
and India, and it feeds more than 1 billion of the
world's poorest citizens. Over the next century, up
to 50 percent of wheat-growing areas are expected
to face drought risks from climate change.

JUDITH REDMOND
Pest Control Without Chemicals

Depending on the season, carrots, cayenne peppers, spinach, beets, basil, red kale, daikon, and dozens of other crops grow in neat rows at Full Belly Farm in northern California's Capay Valley. Year-round, the borders that surround the fields are planted with coyote brush, toyon, yarrow, and other wild bushes and shrubs.

The wiry natives look so scraggly and ordinary next to the lush, green rows of fruits and vegetables that you might not pay much attention to them. But Judith Redmond sure does. As one of four farmer-owners of the 250-acre organic farm, she takes a special interest in the strips of native plants, which are called hedgerows. They provide habitat for ladybugs and lacewings, which eat harmful bugs, and for insects that carry the pollen needed for the crops to produce.

By planting and maintaining hedgerows as a year-round home for beneficial insects, the farmers don't need to spray pesticides on their crops or rely on honeybees, which are often trucked to fields and orchards, to pollinate them.

"We're trying to work with nature to grow our own pest-management and pollinating insects," Redmond says.

The hedgerows are just one of the ways that Full Belly Farm is different from most conventional farms—and even some organic farms. Full Belly meets and often exceeds federal organic standards. "But we also feel that social issues and community issues are an equally important part of the whole balance," Redmond says.

For example, the farm employs a full-time staff of 25 to 30 farm laborers. Some of them have worked at the farm since it started in 1985;

about a dozen have been there for 15 years or longer. Unlike seasonal migrant workers, they are able to send their kids to local schools, purchase homes, and put down roots in the community.

The farm also operates a year-round apprenticeship program, which trains future farmers in organic practices, such as using cover crops that "fix" nitrogen and provide organic matter for the soil.

Redmond grew up in Santa Barbara and has a master's degree in plant pathology from the University of California, Davis. She finds most aspects of farm life fulfilling. "What's really satisfying," she says, "is knowing that at the end of the day, I can look into our coolers here, and see that what we've picked, and packed, and sold is really, really healthy, delicious food that people are going to get tomorrow."

Judith Redmond's September Salad

3 organic Asian pears

1/2 cup walnuts, in approximately 1/4-inch pieces

1/2 tablespoon Balsamic vinegar

1/8 teaspoon sea salt

Several grinds of fresh black pepper

Scant 1/8 cup olive oil

2-3 cups baby arugula leaves, loosely packed

Roast the walnuts 5 minutes or more (until golden) in a 350-degree oven (spread in a layer on a baking sheet) or toss in a small cast-iron pan on medium heat on the stove.

Make a vinaigrette by mixing the vinegar with salt and pepper, then thoroughly whisk in the olive oil. Quarter and core the pears.

Rinse the arugula in a bowl of cold water, drain, dry. When everything else is ready, slice the pears thinly, add them to the arugula, then toss both with the vinaigrette and mix in the walnuts. Ideally, serve immediately, but it's still great after sitting a while.

RICE

Now a staple in the diet of more than 2 billion people around the world, rice has been cultivated for nearly 8,000 years. The oldest known rice paddies were discovered in a coastal swamp in China's Zhejiang Province, near Hangzhou. Fittingly, the Chinese word for rice is *fan*, which also means food. In the Arabian Gulf, rice is called *aish*, which also means life.

The Green Revolution Begins

After World War II, when the United States assumed a leading role in global affairs, it tried to address food shortages in developing countries. To do so, it began to export its industrial-based agricultural methods. This became known as the "Green Revolution." African nations, and India, Mexico, and the Philippines began farming with U.S. seeds, fertilizers, and pesticides—and planting methods.

America's "Green Revolution" alleviated food shortages and produced high crop yields. But it was a temporary solution. In the long run, genetically diverse crops were replaced with a narrow range of wheat and rice varieties. And rotations of crops such as wheat, maize, millet, and seeds grown for their oil were abandoned.

Growing one crop in huge quantities affects not only the immediate planting fields but also the surrounding land. Monocultures choke out native plants and threaten the biological diversity that creates stable ecosystems and fosters stable local economies . When you grow a variety of crops and a disease or pest attacks one of them, others can survive. But when you grow only one crop, a disease or pest can wipe out your entire harvest. Therefore single-crop farmers often rely heavily on chemicals to control insects and protect crops.

> *"We're trying to work with nature to grow our own pest-management and pollinating insects."*
> —JUDITH REDMOND

Critics of the Green Revolution, such as Indian physicist and environmental activist Vindana Shiva, say that the introduction of modern Western agricultural practices and chemicals changed the long-standing traditions, cultures, and ecology of local regions.

RACHEL CARSON
Tying Pesticides to a Birdless Spring

Today most people are aware of how humans impact the health of our planet. Writer and biologist Rachel Carson was the pioneer who started that thinking. In the 1960s, she wrote a book that redefined our responsibility for the natural world. *Silent Spring* focused on the environmental consequences of widespread pesticide use.

In an introduction to a recent edition of *Silent Spring*, former Vice President Al Gore wrote, "Without this book, the environmental movement might have been long delayed or never developed at all."

Silent Spring was inspired by a letter from one of Carson's friends about the spraying of DDT in her town. The pesticide was used to control mosquitoes, but large numbers of birds died following the spraying. Carson researched DDT and learned how it enters the food chain and affects individual organisms, their internal biology, and the overall stability of the ecosystem.

She did not say that all pesticides were bad, as some of her critics contend, but she acknowledged that humankind had a moral responsibility to use pesticides in a way that didn't harm other species.

"The balance of nature is ... a complex, precise, and highly integrated system of relationships between living things which cannot be safely ignored any more than the

© Alfred Eisenstaedt/Time & Life Pictures/Getty Images

laws of gravity can be defied," Carson wrote.

Silent Spring imagines a town where the indiscriminate use of chemicals harms birds, animals, and, ultimately, people. The book and Carson's ideas were seen as radical. At that time, a woman who had chosen a career in science faced great skepticism and even prejudice. Critics called her "hysterical and emotional."

But when *Silent Spring* sold more than half a million copies, influential people took note. President John F. Kennedy read the book and appointed a panel to examine Carson's findings. It agreed with her conclusions. Soon the first environmental organizations were formed.

Carson died of breast cancer 18 months after the publication of *Silent Spring*. Her book, says Al Gore, "planted the seeds of a new activism that has grown into one of the great popular forces of all time."

USING YOUR OWN VOICE

Rachel Carson spoke out and ended up inspiring a movement. What do you see around you that you need to speak out about? How about at your school? When you "go your own way," how does criticism affect you? How do you overcome it?

In the 1960s, Carson was one of the few women in her field. But she persevered and helped all of humanity. In what other ways do you see science as a profession that helps humanity? How would you use science to help the planet?

How would you make your voice heard? What makes you nervous about speaking out?

PESTICIDES AND YOUR FOOD

Various pesticides are used on conventional (nonorganic) food crops around the country. Check out foodnews.org for a list of fruits and vegetables that retain the most pesticide residue. Peaches are at the top of the list; apples are No. 2. The list was developed from U.S. Department of Agriculture data by the not-for-profit Environmental Working Group, which recommends choosing organic whenever possible.

Counting Costs, and Benefits

Solutions to even simple issues are rarely perfect or without consequence. So it's important to weigh the pros and cons of possible outcomes before taking action. Suppose you want to achieve something as seemingly clear-cut as serving more local food in your school cafeteria. You approach local farmers, but the cost is prohibitive. How could you bring down the cost? Could you partner with other schools or institutions in your area to increase the volume of your purchase and possibly get a break on the cost?

The rice terraces of Long Ji in China's Guangxi province date to the 13th century and are called the "Dragon's Backbone."

SOLUTIONS NEAR AND FAR

Changing food systems for improved health (of people and Earth!) is a complex matter.

It involves economics, politics, culture, and tradition—and leadership. Already some brilliant and effective solutions have come about, especially for fighting world hunger and malnutrition.

Using a base of peanuts and powdered milk, ready-to-use-foods make seriously malnourished children healthy again. And the EarthBox, a 1-foot-tall plastic container garden, helps fight famine around the world. The EarthBox needs minimal space, light, and water. It's just 2 ½ feet long and 15 inches wide. Its shower cap–like covering keeps the soil moist, and water is wicked up through the roots rather than seeping down from above. This helps conserve that most valuable resource—water. The EarthBox is the invention of Florida tomato farmer Blake Whisenant.

An urban garden flourishes in Brooklyn's East New York neighborhood, right.

Student EarthBox gardeners in dozens of U.S. cities now connect with young EarthBox farmers around the world, including those in rural villages in Ghana, above, and urban schools in Mexico. They do so through the Growing Connection, a program launched by the United Nations Food and Agriculture Organization and the American Horticultural Society. Nine countries take part in the program, which has students sharing gardening experiences and learning about one another's cultures—while feeding themselves and their families.

Many innovative programs reach around the world to alleviate health and land issues. But many experts now believe that the most effective solutions will come from *within* local communities. This means flipping the model of how change typically occurs, so that ideas and methods rise up from the bottom instead of traveling from the top down. In this way, local wisdom and practices, passed from generation to generation, can be honored and incorporated into long-lasting solutions.

Having looked at a number of rooftop gardens and walls, Detroit-based musician and hunger activist Taja Sevelle and architect Robin Osler put the two together. They wondered: Why not grow tomatoes, peppers, and onions by turning horizontal planting beds into a vertical enterprise? Working with manufacturer George Irwin and Urban Farming's Los Angeles team, they came up with a design for anchoring plants in dirt-filled cells set into stainless steel that could be attached to buildings. In the summer of 2008, they inaugurated their Urban Farming Food Chain at four sites in Los Angeles' Skid Row, one of the city's most underserved neighborhoods. Each 30-foot-long, 6-foot-high wall contains 4,000 plants. Other designers have plans for vertical farming towers in urban centers so that the food production takes place where there is the greatest demand.

> *"If you start with something small, you can always make it bigger."*
> — IVY VANCE

And then there's the bicycle blender. It's just what it sounds like: a blender rigged to the fender of a bicycle, powered by the person pedaling. That's exercise and nutrition in one! Students in Philadelphia's Urban Nutrition Initiative set up a bike-blender smoothie stand right in their high school.

LADONNA REDMOND
Caring for Community

The Institute for Community Resource Development, founded in Chicago by LaDonna Redmond, is all about community. The organization not only grows food for the local community but also employs that community to plant and harvest, transport compost, and do short-term construction.

"There's an intellect that's already in the community, and once it's tapped into, people can solve their own problems," Redmond says.

One of the first problems Redmond wanted to solve was finding organic foods for her young son, who had food allergies. Organic produce wasn't sold at stores in her West Side neighborhood. In other neighborhoods, it was too expensive. So she and her family started a garden.

Redmond grew up volunteering at church, at food pantries, and in several well-known Chicago social justice and political campaigns. She spent time at Operation PUSH (People United to Serve Humanity). The organization was started by the Rev. Jesse Jackson.

In her work, Redmond stays attuned to others. "I was always taught to listen to people's stories," she says. "I keep coming back to work that opens the heart and connects people in a different way. For me to come in with 'my answer' is not necessarily the way to build community. I may have part of the answer and you may have part of the answer and together we may be able to come up with a solution that's unique and beneficial, where there is an openness to the process that allows everyone to be involved."

Sharing food, says Redmond, is one of the most joyous ways to bring people together. "I am always prepared to create commonality through food," she says.

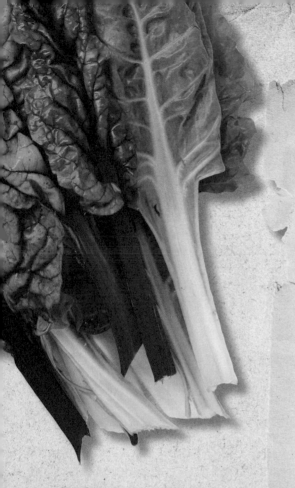

"I just love greens," LaDonna Redmond says. "I love to watch them grow. They grow quickly and are pretty plants. I am not sure why, but my favorites are spinach and rainbow Swiss chard."

Stir-Fried Swiss Chard

4–6 servings

1 teaspoon toasted sesame oil

1 onion, chopped

Green peppers or other add-in vegetables, also chopped (optional)

3 bunches Swiss chard (or other greens of your choice), washed, dried, and cut width-wise across the leaf, down to the stem (If you're feeling adventurous, add in the stems.)

1/2 cup of water

Sprinkle of salt

Onion or garlic powder, or 2 cloves of chopped garlic (optional)

Pour the oil in skillet and turn heat to medium. Add onions and cook until clear. Add peppers or other optional vegetables and cook a few minutes. Add Swiss chard and stir until it is coated with the oil. Cook until slightly tender. Add the water and any other seasoning you like, such as onion powder, fresh garlic, or garlic powder. Cover skillet, lower the heat, and simmer for 15–20 minutes, stirring and tasting occasionally until th e greens reach the texture you prefer—crunchy to tender.

WHOM ARE YOU SHARING FOOD WITH?

Who organizes the food in your home? What shopping routine do you follow? Is your family adventurous about trying new tastes? You're in the vanguard of creating a new food culture, a way of reconnecting your family, your community, and yourself to the production and preparation of food. How are you using what you have learned about food to educate others?

MARY CATHERINE MUNIZ
Recipes That Work

Mary Catherine Muniz wrote "Delectable Dishes for Less," a recipe booklet for food-bank clients, after being inspired by a newspaper article about the rise in families seeking assistance from food banks and food pantries.

Drawing on her family's Cuban-American heritage, Muniz, of West Linn, Oregon, cooked up meal suggestions that use ingredients commonly distributed by food pantries, including beans, canned tuna, and bread.

Muniz, now a student at Macalester College in Minnesota, says the project made her realize that food doesn't have to be expensive or complicated to be delicious. Muniz hadn't cooked much before her project. She borrowed from her family's traditional recipes, her mom's collection, and the food page of her local newspaper.

The project earned Muniz a Girl Scout Gold Award, and it has had a much greater impact than she expected. Her booklet has been requested by food pantries in Washington State and California, and a blog entry about it caught the eye of a writer for a German magazine for students learning English. So "Delectable Dishes for Less" is enjoying a global reach.

Pantry volunteers report that the recipes have been well received and are producing appetizing results. Two are featured on the next page. The first turned Muniz into a fan of beets. The second— Muniz's favorite—comes from a Polish friend of her mom's. "It sounded like a dessert with such a strange combination of ingredients, I just had to try baking them," she says. "I love how the cookies have a subtle, savory flavor along with the sweet and cinnamon tastes."

Applesauce and Cheese Cookies

3/4 cup sugar (divided)

2 1/2 cups flour

1/2 teaspoon salt

3/4 cups butter or real margarine, softened (look for one that says it is for cooking and doesn't have too much water)

1/3 cup sweetened applesauce

1/2 teaspoon vanilla

1/2 cup shredded cheddar cheese

1/2 teaspoon cinnamon

Preheat the oven to 350 degrees. In a large bowl, mix 1/2 cup sugar, flour, salt, butter, applesauce, and vanilla until smooth. Stir in cheese. Roll the dough into balls that are an inch in diameter. Roll each ball in a mixture of the cinnamon and remaining 1/4 cup of sugar. Place the balls on a buttered cooking sheet and press them with the tines of a fork. Bake for 14 to 17 minutes. Makes about 3 dozen.

Beet Salad

3 tablespoons olive oil

2 pinches salt

1 pinch pepper

1 clove garlic, minced

1/2 of a medium orange, juiced

1 (15-ounce) can sliced beets, or 3–4 medium beets cooked until tender and then sliced

Mix olive oil, salt, pepper, garlic, and the juice of the orange in a small bowl. Pour over beets. Makes 3–4 servings.

MIRIAM MANION
City Farms, City Food

Miriam Manion had never eaten collard or mustard greens until the food bank she worked for partnered with a local farmer to grow them. "It just kind of broadened my world to what's available," the Pittsburgh native says.

Now, as executive director of Grow Pittsburgh, Manion helps expand the selection of fresh vegetables grown and sold in the city.

Grow Pittsburgh is a nonprofit organization that operates urban farms and develops community gardens. "The big benefit of a garden is that it makes fresh fruits and vegetables available to city residents who might not otherwise have locally grown produce," Manion says.

"Where Braddock Farms is, there are no grocery stores," she adds, referring to a farm on a series of abandoned lots near the last remaining steel mill in the historic borough of Braddock. The farm is the area's only access to fresh produce. "So that means a lot," Manion says.

The greening of Pittsburgh is due in part to the erosion of the region's manufacturing base. The city has 14,000 vacant lots, which Grow Pittsburgh taps for community gardens. Grow Pittsburgh also works with public schools to teach kids to grow and eat healthy foods, and it runs a summer internship program that puts local teenagers to work on farms.

What Manion likes most is working with the interns and other young people involved in the sustainable farming movement. "They're so committed to a world that is different than the world as it is now," she says.

KAREN BLAINE
Reconnecting with Culture

For the Tohono O'odham Nation, which has lived for thousands of years on desert land in what is now southern Arizona, food and cultural values are inextricably linked. Their songs, stories, and legends revolve around agriculture, explains Karen Blaine, program coordinator for Tohono O'odham Community Action (TOCA). One O'odham story, passed from generation to generation, connects Earth and sky by way of a coyote who throws a handful of white tepary beans in the air so that they become the Milky Way.

Tepary beans, a traditional Tohono O'odham food, have an intense, nutty flavor. They thrive in desert conditions. They're also high in protein, and they help regulate blood sugar levels, which is especially beneficial to people with diabetes.

The Tohono O'odham lived for centuries with these foods. But over the last half century, processed foods began to undermine their agricultural

and dietary practices. They now suffer from one of the highest rates of diabetes and obesity in the world.

Blaine holds workshops to reconnect her people with their traditional foods. The local hospital now serves teparies and so do three regional schools. Other traditional foods, gathered in the wild, include cholla buds from cacti, which are sun-dried, and mesquite beans and pods. TOCA addresses the needs of its own community—they have a store and plan to open a café— and they also sell to nearby resorts and spas.

Lost and Found
What healthful traditions or foods have been lost in your community? How might you bring them back?

DENISE O'BRIEN
An Oasis of Biodiversity in a Sea of Corn and Soy

Denise O'Brien has always seen herself as a grassroots activist. But the community that she fights for expands beyond her hometown to the global agricultural community. O'Brien is a farmer, a family-farm advocate, a food-security policy activist, and a voice for women farmers at home and around the globe. In 2006, she was a candidate for Iowa's Secretary of Agriculture.

In the 1980s, when thousands of U.S. family farms were stressed, sold, or bankrupt, O'Brien became involved in a farm advocacy group. She held workshops on women and agriculture at the 1995 United Nations Conference on Women, in Beijing, and took 35 women from 29 countries to the World Food Summit in Rome. She has met with women farmers all over the world and says she has always felt a deep connection, and solidarity, with their hard work and struggle. "When you get together with women of the land, you can see that we all have hands that are calloused," O'Brien says. "There is a camaraderie."

In 1997, she launched the Women, Food and Agriculture Network, which now has a membership of 150 women. "We have workshops on how to clean a chain saw or get a tractor ready for winter," says O'Brien. "And we also get together just to be with each other, to sit and talk and share our experiences of what the farming year is like." As you might expect, their celebrations include food.

For more than 20 years, O'Brien and her husband, Larry Harris, grew soy and corn, and raised beef cattle and then dairy

cows on more than 300 acres. Their now-scaled-down 16-acre Rolling Acres Farm, outside Atlantic, Iowa, is part of a national community-supported agriculture system (CSA). A CSA is a farm in which local families buy shares to support the farm operation in exchange for a portion of the weekly harvest. About 20 families share the farm's bounty: apples, strawberries, raspberries, watermelon, asparagus, pumpkin, peppers, and lettuce.

   "Our farm looks like an oasis in a county that grows just corn and soy," O'Brien says. "Every square inch of Iowa has been modified to accommodate food. We feel responsible about maintaining biodiversity."

   Working the land to produce food has been a journey toward clarity for O'Brien, one that ultimately led to her advocacy. "I'm out there in the fields working by myself for entire days, so you think things over a lot," she says. "Farming has helped me process my thoughts, and that's what's made me articulate."

Denise O'Brien's Kohlrabi Slaw

"I like this recipe," says O'Brien, "not only because it tastes so good but because it also uses a vegetable that is easy and fast to grow. Kohlrabi takes about 50 days to grow, which is relatively fast, though not as fast as radishes at 25 days! The recipe is also fast to make and delicious on a hot summer day."

1 large kohlrabi, peeled and grated

1/2 apple, peeled and grated

1 carrot, peeled and grated

1/2 sweet yellow or red onion, thinly sliced

Handful of parsley, leaves only

Juice of half a lime

3 or 4 shakes of sherry wine vinegar (place thumb over bottle opening and shake)

2 tablespoons mayonnaise, or enough to bind ingredients

Sea salt and fresh pepper to taste

Combine everything in a large bowl. Mix well. Chill 30 minutes to allow the flavors to blend before serving.

ANDREIA BORGES
Making the Most of the Land

Andreia Borges' mother and father were migrant workers on coffee plantations. No one in her family had ever owned land. Now Borges is part of a new generation of farmers and rural land reformers in Brazil. For the last 12 years, she and her husband, along with 15 other families, have been growing most of their own food on eight acres in Santa Catarina province on Brazil's southern coast.

Nearly a quarter of Brazil's 186 million people live below the poverty line. The main city, Rio de Janeiro, is known for its vast slums, or *favelas*. The goal of collective farming is to establish reasonable self-sufficiency—and a steady stream of income.

Borges' collective grows 16 types of organic vegetables, including three kinds of lettuce, arugula, spinach, radicchio, scallions, and parsley. It also produces beans and corn and has eggs, cows for milk and cheese, and six aquaculture tanks for raising fish. This bounty is sold to nearby supermarkets and sidewalk food stands.

"Peasant families," says Borges, "have a very intimate relationship with the food they eat. For us, corn is not just corn. It's part of our daily living."

Borges is a member of the Landless Workers Movement. The organization sets its sights on occupying agricultural land that is not in production or not slated for another use. This redistribution of land to ordinary citizens is based on the new Brazilian Constitution written in the mid-1980s after 30 years of dictatorship. A clause in the constitution states

that "all land must be productive."

More than half a million families have benefited from the Landless Workers Movement. Women have been organizing and making decisions from the very beginning. "Women bring a special quality to the work," Borges says. "Women provide consistency, pay attention to details, and have a great capacity for sacrifice. For women, the land is not a business."

Women and their daughters also play a key role in the cultural life of the farming collectives. Group meetings are ceremoniously opened and closed with social dramas known as *misticas*, which are reflections on recent events; they're also a way to galvanize and motivate members. *Misticas* may include spoken word, art, poetry, and silent performance; they're often based on women's relationship with seeds and their capacity to produce food and life.

"We decorate the stage with food: bread, seeds, stalks of corn, branches, and grasses," Borges says. Sometimes pregnant women hand out seeds or give people small pieces of earth. "We want to do something evocative to inspire people."

Borges sees the next generation, reared on the collective, as having a different outlook on life. The curriculum they are taught, she says, includes lessons on the land. "The children grow stuff and they see a connection between the cycle of crops and the cycle of school. They are healthy; they communicate more and are freer. Even small children are able to discuss politics and analyze!"

SARAH SCHWENNESEN
Raising Corn-Free Cows

Sarah Schwennesen says she doesn't need TV—she can watch the chickens on her family's cattle ranch strut and cluck, peck and scratch for bugs, and take baths in the dirt. They're endless fun—and a reminder of the natural cycle of life on Double Check Ranch, which produces hormone-free, grass-fed beef. "It feels very harmonious," Schwennesen says.

The cows that Schwennesen, her husband, Paul, and Paul's parents raise 60 miles north of Tucson, Arizona, are not fed corn or other grains. They don't receive protein supplements, antibiotics, or growth hormones. Instead, they graze and forage freely on the open range of the 14,000-acre ranch. Then they're moved to irrigated pastures to fatten some more.

It takes about twice as long to raise grass-fed cattle as it does to raise grain-fed cows. Many people believe that the end result is healthier, better-tasting beef that is higher in omega-3 fatty acids and richer in nutrients and antioxidants, including vitamin E and beta carotene. "For our burgers, we just do salt and pepper to season and then grill them up," Schwennesen says.

"I'm glad when I look out on our pasture and see our cows, I can say they will never go to a feedlot, and they will never go to a huge slaughterhouse," she adds.

Schwennesen grew up in the suburbs of Golden, Colorado. One surprise about ranch life was seeing how quickly fences, machinery, and things in general wear out or break down. Sometimes it's the cows who do the breaking. "Cows seem to be a lot like toddlers," Schwennesen says. "They're big animals, and they're curious. They break a lot of things!"

So, what about values?

As you can see by now, when you want to improve your food print to better the world's food network, it all comes down to what decisions you're willing to make. And, of course, your decisions are tied to your values—and your willingness to stand by them.

Think about all the values of the Girl Scout Law and how many of them the women profiled throughout this journey are living. Using resources wisely, being courageous and strong, making the world a better place—all of these and more are reflected in the way women pursue their ties to the food network and larger issues of food and land use.

Which women and which values do you admire most? Which value do you think is the hardest to live up to?

There's no one right answer. What speaks to you? Compare your thoughts with those of your friends.

HARVEST AWARD
Fields of Possibilities

Now that you've seen what the food network does for you, what will you do for it?

Get your leader print going! Here's the path:

1 **Identify, and dig into, a food or land issue, tapping some community experts as you go.**

Maybe you've met growers, gardeners, nutritionists or others in your region and have ideas about challenges they face. Maybe you've improved your food print and want to inspire others. Want your school to host a farmers' market? Got a seed of an idea from this book? Want to team up with other Seniors? Just choose an issue that allows you to use your unique talents and learn something new, too!

Fruit and flower sellers maneuver through a floating market in Bangkok, Thailand.

Capture your vision for change in a Harvest Plan that includes:

Your very own "So What?"—your goal, why it matters, how it will benefit both the planet and people. Say it in a way that gets others interested and involved! Show how even simple actions and decisions impact the larger food network.

Remember: No need to go it alone. Who can you turn to for input and support?

What specific impact do you hope to have? Name it! And when you have executed your plan, check back. Have you achieved it? Maybe you will have achieved other results, too, especially if you find yourself needing to adjust your plans along the way.

A good project plan...

 gives you the opportunity to expand your network...

 is realistic based on your time and interest...

 uses your unique skills and talents...

 helps you learn something you can apply to your life...

 contributes to sustainable change.

Your project can be big or small, depending on your time and interest. Either way, strive for a sustainable impact. You may push for a new policy or for a change in an existing one. You don't need to start something from scratch.

3

Now, create change—execute your plan by influencing a food policy or land-use effort (yes, you can!), or by educating and inspiring others to act on a solution you identify.

Get going! And while you're at it:

✦ Take time to stop and think along the way. Do you need to adjust anything based on new information you're learning? Are any new challenges arising?

✦ Be sure to ask adults in your network for success tips! Incorporate the best methods and styles into your own work.

✦ Take time for reflection. What are you doing that surprises you? Are you speaking up more? Solving a problem you thought you couldn't? Take pride in how you are growing.

✦ Think about your team, too. Are you happy with the way everyone is working together? Is there anything you need to talk about? Courageous conversation, anyone?

✦ Who have you educated and inspired to take action along with you? That matters because more people in the know means your impact can have a wide reach!

OPTION: DECLARE IT!

If influencing public policy interests you, you might drum up even more interest in your project by writing a Declaration of the Right to Food. Plenty of official declarations name food as a basic human right. Once you've written your declaration, work with local leaders to get it adopted by your community. Practice presenting it, anticipate questions, and then ask to be on the agenda of an upcoming meeting of your governing body.

HERE ARE SOME IDEAS TO GET YOU BRAINSTORMING YOUR OWN UNIQUE PROJECT.

Promote Access and Use of Local Produce

ENLIST some support. Who really cares about this issue and could give you some great advice, maybe even connect you with those already involved in an issue to which you can contribute? Food proprietors? Restaurateurs who use local food sources?

Help get **PLANS** under way in your neighborhood for local food producers to sell their goods. Can they sell at a school, library, some other place? What's needed? Perhaps an existing market needs help attracting more customers.

Get **RESTAURANTS** or **GROCERS** to carry local produce, at least sometimes. Or they might hold special monthly events on local foods.

Who can help you **MEASURE** the impact of your project? The local chamber of commerce? A government economic office?

Develop some simple **RECIPES**, using local produce, to share at your planning meetings and, ultimately, at the location of your project.

Eliminate Food Waste

The United States produces a lot of waste, perhaps 40 percent of the world's waste output. At times, more than 30 percent of that waste is food! Not only is it a moral issue that people with more than enough food throw some of it out when it could be redistributed to people who are hungry, but rotting food scraps emit greenhouse gases that contribute to climate change. Some restaurants are actually starting to charge for food that is left on your plate! So what can you do?

Explore all your avenues! Here are some examples of projects that can help reduce food waste:

If you *focus* on your school CAFETERIA, talk to those in charge. Where does the waste go? Can you reduce that waste? Can it be turned into compost? Consider partnering with a local farmer or urban farming initiative that will accept the food waste into its existing compost stream. Can your project expand to multiple schools?

If you *focus* on RESTAURANTS, survey how they handle food portions and waste. You might even ask if you and your team can spend one night (or several!) photographing diners' plates at the end of a meal. The results might lead you to seek local legislation requiring restaurants to offer half-portions and allow sharing of portions without "extra plate" charges.

If you *focus* on PRIVATE HOUSEHOLDS, you might create a public compost site where families can bring their food scraps. In New York City, citizens can bring food waste to the Union Square Greenmarket for composting instead of putting it in the city's waste stream.

As you *focus* on EDUCATING others, you might create a photo gallery or some other creative way to show people what we waste. Then get them to commit to reducing that waste!

Inspire Others to Change Their Food Prints, Too!

Imagine if everyone you know made a change or two or 10. Here are some ways:

PRODUCE a Community Food Guide that gives people a base of knowledge of where to find good foods. Your guide can inform people about all the places where food can be purchased, including producers selling directly to consumers. Identify all sources of local food. Spotlight cultural offerings and ethnic markets. Show others how to calculate their food print, too! (Be mindful of resources! Keep any paper use in check!)

Put your guide in the SPOTLIGHT by unveiling it during a community food tour that you organize. Work with supermarkets, shop owners, farmers' markets, and producers. Include cooking demos and smart shopping tips, including how to read labels.

SCOUT the best locations in your community and find out how to get permission to use the property. Does your town have an existing program for starting community gardens? Is the soil ready? Your County Agricultural Extension Service and its master gardeners are good resources for soil testing. Learn what grows well in the soil. Include native plants.

If planning a school garden, SEEK support from teachers, parents, administrators, and custodial staff. What tools, time, and space can they offer? Meet with the school dietician and/or food service about using the garden's bounty at school. Or share your harvest with community members who have limited access to healthy food.

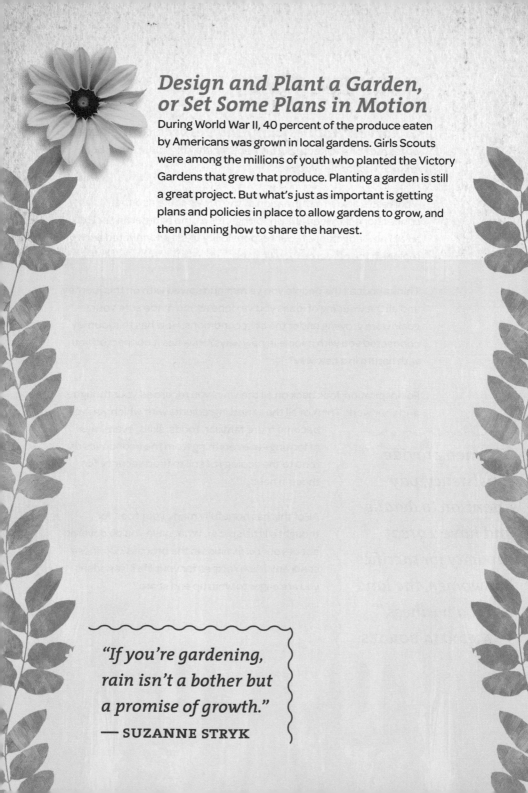

Design and Plant a Garden, or Set Some Plans in Motion

During World War II, 40 percent of the produce eaten by Americans was grown in local gardens. Girls Scouts were among the millions of youth who planted the Victory Gardens that grew that produce. Planting a garden is still a great project. But what's just as important is getting plans and policies in place to allow gardens to grow, and then planning how to share the harvest.

"If you're gardening, rain isn't a bother but a promise of growth."

— **SUZANNE STRYK**

HARVEST TIME!

"A harvest implies planning, respect, and effort," writes author and Kentucky farmer Barbara Kingsolver in her book *Animal, Vegetable, Miracle.*

A harvest is also a reaffirmation of the cycles of life and the connections between all living things. It's a time of receiving and also an acknowledgment of your responsibility to stay connected and to replenish the resources you've used.

Think about all the people you've met and sowed with on this journey, and all the weeding of ideas you've done as you made sure your goals were growing under the best conditions. How has this journey connected you with people in new ways? How has it connected you with nature in a new way?

For inspiration, look back on all the ways you recorded your thoughts and your work. Think of all the varied ingredients with which you've become more familiar: foods, skills, even ways of looking—at everything from the economics of food to the ecology of soil to food security for those in need.

"Women provide consistency, pay attention to details, and have a great capacity for sacrifice. For women, the land is not a business."
— **ANDREIA BORGES**

All of this has hopefully made your food for thought a little spicier. What have you discovered about your own values in the process? Do these spark any fresh recipes for your life? New ideas you are eager to whip up and share?

Give Thanks for Your Bounty

Think back on your personal food network. Start with your favorite food. Picture all the people involved in getting it to you. Who are they and where do they live? What is their workday like? Who loaded your food on the truck, ship, or plane? What's in their daily diet? Can you find ways to be thankful to each person?

Now, go seek them out and give a personal thank you to all you can. Start with the person who buys the groceries at your house. Then thank your supermarket manager and meat and produce managers, or the person who runs your local convenience market. Don't forget about the farmer and the farm workers! As you thank each member of your network, how do you feel? Do you feel more connected to your community? What values and personal resources do those in your food network add to your life?

A FRESH FOOD WEB FOR YOUR FUTURE

Can you imagine a food network that incorporates not only how energy and nutrients are passed along but also how values are transmitted?

Along this journey, you figured out some new ideas about your food print and used your leader print to get others involved in seeds of change for the food network.

You also DISCOVERED ways to live your values. You may have even shifted your values, too.

You certainly CONNECTED with others who live their values and who have, over time, shifted some of their values.

So, what will you TAKE ACTION on next? How will you apply your values to all the new crops you want to sow and all the new bounty you hope to harvest?

As you plow forward, you'll see that the best thing about a network is that you can continue to build it from the inside out. You can keep on having an impact—always and forever! The changes you make for yourself and others mean positive change for the planet, too.